T0299573

Cover: All photographs
© Orange Hippo, with the exception
of background texture (© Antpkr/
Shutterstock)

Published in 2019 by Orange Hippo
20 Mortimer Street
London W1T 3JW

Text © Orange Hippo 2019
Design © Orange Hippo 2019

A CIP catalogue record for this book
is available from the British Library.

ISBN 978 1 78739 330 1

10 9 8 7 6 5 4 3 2 1

Printed in Dubai

WHERE Doves CRAFT

10 Projects Inspired by the Artist

OH!

Contents

INTRODUCTION: About the Artist

10

Prince FINGER PUPPET

The spirit of Prince at your fingertips

14

I WOULD *Dye* FOR YOU

Try the craft
formerly known as batik

20

PURPLE *Crane*

I only want to see you laughing
with your purple crane

26

Raspberry CROCHET

Not the kind you find in
a second-hand store

32

YOU GOT THE *Scrapbook*

A cut-out-and-keep
Prince to stick in your fan album

38

NO PARTICULAR *Sign*

Create a handpainted sign for your home

44

Snow IN APRIL

Try your hand at seasonal papercraft

50

YOUR EXTRA TIME AND YOUR *Stitch*

Cross-stitch your favourite lyrics

56

Macramé YOUR MAMA HAPPY

With this sensational wall hanging

62

Whittle RED CROCHET HOOK

Woodwork a love that's gonna last

70

76 TEMPLATES | **90** TIMELINE

93 INDEX | **96** CREDITS

Introduction

There's no denying that Prince was a musical genius – we've all heard his songs played on the radio, watched his music videos, or even been lucky enough to see him performing on stage. He wrote music and lyrics, as well as playing numerous instruments and, of course, singing vocals. But his creativity wasn't limited to the musical arena. From his sanctuary at Paisley Park, Prince explored design and colour, decorating the space with everything from plush purple velvet sofas to a "galaxy room" in which to practice meditation. In the same way that Prince blended musical styles, he also combined design, pattern, and colour, creating his own signature look that was as unique and kooky as he was. A true individual, we can learn a lot from Prince about doing our own thing and creating our own path in life.

In this book we have showcased projects that use a range of craft materials and skills, to allow you to be creative, experiment, and try new things. We've paid homage to Prince not only as a musical icon, but also as an icon of creativity and self-expression. Although we can't all be musical geniuses like he was, through crafting we can attempt to bring a touch of his flair and style into our lives.

Recently, there has been a lot of talk around the mental and physical benefits of exploring creativity through crafting objects by hand. There is something so intrinsically satisfying about making something with your hands – the sense of accomplishment when you finish a project and can proudly say "I made that", and the feeling of being so totally absorbed in a task that you don't realize how much time has passed. It's this feeling of absorption and complete focus on the task in hand that draws so many people to creative activities – perhaps it was even this that drove Prince to live the intensely creative life that he did. In this book, we have combined our love of crafts with our deeply held love of Prince to create 10 fun projects that we hope will inspire you, and spark your creativity.

Sonia & Zoe, London Craft Club

Projects

The spirit of Prince at your fingertips

Prince changed our lives back in 1984. Totally sexy and wildly experimental, *Purple Rain* the album, tour and film were like nothing we'd seen before. Here was the story of Prince's life – and it rocked!

From that moment on, everyone knew Prince and, what's more, they knew what he looked like. He used the power of frills, smoke and purple to catch our attention, although sometimes his outré style slightly overshadowed his musicianship. But there's no denying his creative and technical virtuosity, so we've made sure that our Prince Finger Puppet has his guitar. See if you can capture the way he held it when you stitch it in place. Take a little time to embellish it with anything extra you think he'd have enjoyed, adding lace or organza to really ramp up the ruffles.

YOU WILL NEED:

- Black, purple and a skin-tone felt (one small sheet of each)
- Scissors
- Thread in black, purple, white and a skin tone
- Stiff white fabric (for his shirt)
- A needle
- Pins
- Pattern template printed on paper (see page 79)

1. Cut out the coloured shapes from the pattern (see page 79), and pin them to the pieces of felt. Don't forget to cut out two guitars. Make sure the pins don't stick out over the edge of the paper or you'll ruin your scissors when you cut them out.

2. Using your scissors, cut out the shapes from the felt and white shirt fabric. Sharp fabric scissors make this a lot easier, but you can do it with any scissors you have.

3. Lay the two jacket sides onto Prince's body, and tuck the white shirt parts under the edges of the collar and the sleeves. Pin it all together and stitch it in place using purple thread (we've used a basic running stitch here). Don't forget to add frilly cuffs to both the front and back.

4 Pin the back of Prince's jacket on and use purple thread to stitch the front and back together along the sides of his body and arms. We've used whipstitch (blanket stitch) here.

5 Pin the front and back of Prince's hair in position and use black thread to sew the pieces together in the same way you did for the jacket. Be respectful – Prince hated strangers touching his hair.

6 Put the two pieces of guitar together and stitch all the way around it with black thread. You can stuff some cotton wool or lentils inside the guitar to make it firmer if you like.

7 Cut out your templates for Prince's neckpiece out of the white fabric and layer them up, pinning and then stitching into place at the top with white thread.

Get shirty

The costume designers on *Purple Rain*, Louis Wells and Marie France, were inspired by seventeenth-century shirting to create his frothy, ruffled shirt.

8 Use black thread to stitch a pair of eyes, and a skin-tone thread to stitch his hands in place on the guitar. We used a French knot for his eyes but just a few little stitches will do the job too. Your Prince Finger Puppet is ready to rock!

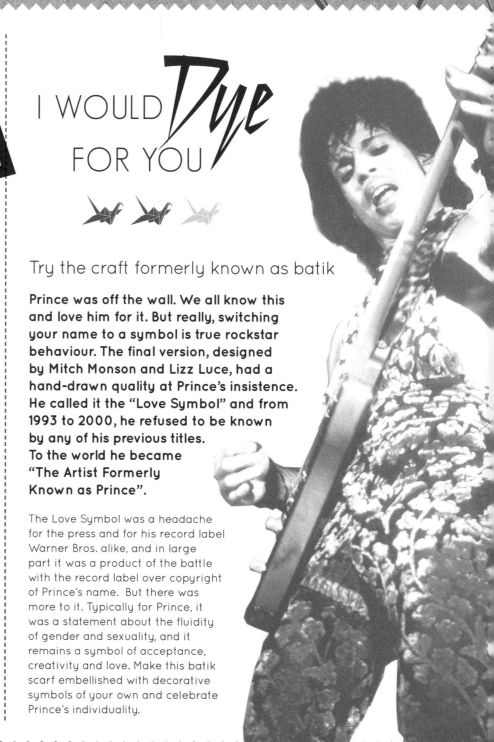

I WOULD *Dye* FOR YOU

Try the craft formerly known as batik

YOU WILL NEED:

- A plain white cotton scarf (lightweight)
- 50g (1 ¾ oz) beeswax pellets
- A thin paintbrush
- A small saucepan
- A plastic tub
- Purple cold dye (hot dye will not work)
- Washing-up gloves
- Kitchen roll
- An iron
- Symbol template printed on paper (see page 81)

Prince was off the wall. We all know this and love him for it. But really, switching your name to a symbol is true rockstar behaviour. The final version, designed by Mitch Monson and Lizz Luce, had a hand-drawn quality at Prince's insistence. He called it the "Love Symbol" and from 1993 to 2000, he refused to be known by any of his previous titles. To the world he became "The Artist Formerly Known as Prince".

The Love Symbol was a headache for the press and for his record label Warner Bros. alike, and in large part it was a product of the battle with the record label over copyright of Prince's name. But there was more to it. Typically for Prince, it was a statement about the fluidity of gender and sexuality, and it remains a symbol of acceptance, creativity and love. Make this batik scarf embellished with decorative symbols of your own and celebrate Prince's individuality.

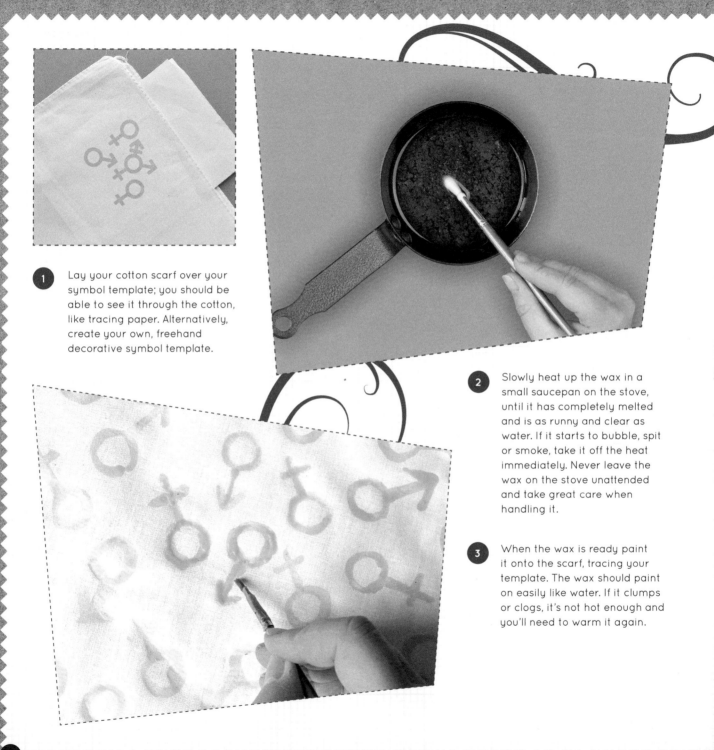

1 Lay your cotton scarf over your symbol template; you should be able to see it through the cotton, like tracing paper. Alternatively, create your own, freehand decorative symbol template.

2 Slowly heat up the wax in a small saucepan on the stove, until it has completely melted and is as runny and clear as water. If it starts to bubble, spit or smoke, take it off the heat immediately. Never leave the wax on the stove unattended and take great care when handling it.

3 When the wax is ready paint it onto the scarf, tracing your template. The wax should paint on easily like water. If it clumps or clogs, it's not hot enough and you'll need to warm it again.

4 Some of the wax will seep through the headscarf and onto the paper below. Peel the headscarf off the paper, move it to a new position and paint on another symbol in wax. You will need to keep reheating the wax. If your brush is clogged with wax, just hold the bristles in the hot wax. Watch it melt away and the brush soften again.

5 When you have finished painting on the wax, leave it to cool and harden. You can crunch it up a little to get the crackled batik effect, but don't let the wax crack off completely.

6 Wearing washing-up gloves, mix your dye in the plastic tub according to the instructions on the packet. Carefully lower in the scarf and leave it to soak for 20 minutes.

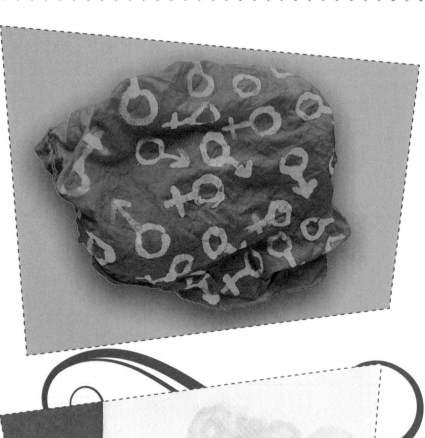

7   Still wearing gloves, remove the scarf from the tub and rinse it under the cold tap. Be careful not to drip the dye, as it can stain clothes and surfaces. When the water runs clear, leave the scarf to dry.

8   When it's dry, place two sheets of paper towel under the scarf and two on top. ron the scarf through the paper towel, and watch the wax soak into the towel. Keep ironing until no more wax comes off. The fabric will be quite stiff from the wax, but if you want you can wash it at 30 degrees and it will soften up.

PURPLE *Crane*

YOU WILL NEED:

- Squares of paper (any size and any colour – but preferably purple!)
- Needle
- Thread
- Purple paint (emulsion or acrylic)
- Glue gun
- Wooden embroidery hoop

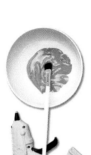

I just want to see you laughing with your purple crane

Purple has long been known as the colour of royalty, but no royal has ever done the colour justice as Prince has done.

Back in 1984 when the *Purple Rain* album, film and single were released, his ownership of the colour was comprehensively confirmed. He chose the colour with good reason. Throughout history, purple had become an emblem of royalty, mainly because it was such an expensive dye to make. Nowadays, it's associated with indulgence, luxury, mystery and sensuality, so of course it would be Prince's colour.

In this next craft, you can make it rain purple cranes. Go for a selection of purple papers and really explore the hue – the more cranes you make, the better.

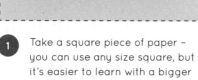

1 Take a square piece of paper – you can use any size square, but it's easier to learn with a bigger piece to start with!

2 Fold the paper in half diagonally, then open it up and fold diagonally the other way. You should have an X-shaped fold across your paper.

3 Flip the paper over so you're working on the opposite side. Fold in half horizontally and open up again, then fold in half vertically to create creases in an eight-pointed star shape.

4 Rotate the paper 45 degrees so that it is a diamond, then bring the left and right points of the diamond together. At the same time, the top and bottom points should automatically fold inwards and come together. This creates an origami "square base".

5 Turn your square 45 degrees so that it is a diamond. Make sure the open part of the folds are at the bottom.

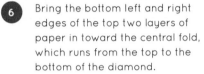

6 Bring the bottom left and right edges of the top two layers of paper in toward the central fold, which runs from the top to the bottom of the diamond.

7 Repeat on the other side, so you end up with a kite shape.

8 Unfold the side you just folded in. At the bottom of the kite, take the top layer of paper and pull it up and back, drawing the sides in as you go. You'll need to reverse some of the creases you've made.

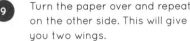

9 Turn the paper over and repeat on the other side. This will give you two wings.

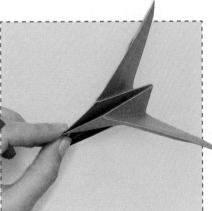

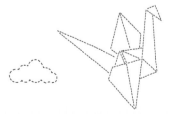

10 Fold the bottom left edge into the centre crease.

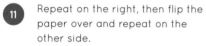

11 Repeat on the right, then flip the paper over and repeat on the other side.

12 Fold the bottom left prong backward and forward to create a crease. Reverse the crease along the length of the prong, and fold inwards and upwards to create the crane's tail.

13 Repeat on the other side to create the neck.

14 Halfway down the neck, create a reverse fold for the head.

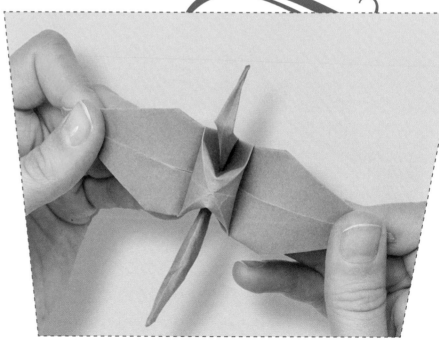

15 Fold the two side sections down to create wings.

16 Take sewing thread and a needle, and thread through the centre of your crane from bottom to top. Thread as many cranes as you want on to each piece of thread. Add a tiny drop of glue from a glue gun where the thread comes out of each crane, just to stop it sliding to the bottom of the thread.

17 Take the inner circle of a wooden embroidery hoop and paint it purple. To create your mobile, hang as many lengths of cranes as you like from the hoop, and it is ready to be displayed.

Video:

Raspberry CROCHET

No second-hand beret to be found? Crochet your own!

Arguably Prince's most perfect pop song, "Raspberry Beret", was released in 1985 on *Around the World in a Day*. It was an instant, worldwide hit and remains a pop anthem and radio favourite nearly 30 years on.

In Prince's typical inimitable style, the girl in the beret who steals his heart is sturdy and not too bright, but rather rebellious nonetheless. If you've been scouring the second-hand stores for a raspberry beret but come up empty handed, you could just crochet one of your own. According to Prince, when the weather is warm, this is all you'll need to wear anyway.

You'll need a 5.5 mm (I-9) crochet hook and a basic knowledge of crochet to create this slouchy hat – the pattern uses US crochet terms. If you're new to crochet, no problem! Use the QR code above, which will lead you to instructional videos on the London Craft Club website.

The first ch3 of each round counts as a dc.
At the end of each round sl st to join, and then sl st
around until you reach the first chain space.

1 Ch, and join with sl st to first ch to form a ring.

2 Ch3 (counts as first dc), 1dc into ring. *Ch1, 2dc* five times. Ch1 and sl st to join.

3 Work into chain space between the pairs of dc. Ch3, dc, ch1, 2dc into first space. *2dc, ch1, 2dc* into each of the other spaces.

4 Ch3, 2dc into first space. *Ch1, 3dc* in each space.

5 Repeat step 4.

6 Repeat step 4.

7 Ch3, dc, ch1, 2dc into first space. *2dc, ch1, 2dc* in each space.

8　Ch3, 2dc into first space. *Ch1, 3dc* in each space.

9　Repeat step 8.

10　Ch3, 2dc into first space. *In next space ch1, 3dc, ch1, then into following space 3dc, ch1, 3dc*. Repeat to the end.

11　Ch3, 2dc into first space. *Ch1, 3dc* in each space.

12　Repeat round 11.

13　Repeat round 11.

14　Ch3, 2dc into first space. *Ch1, 3dc* into each of the next two spaces, then ch1, 3dc, ch1, 3dc into following space. Repeat to the end.

15　Ch3, 2dc into first space. *Ch1, 3dc* in each space.

16　Ch2 *hdc in next two stitches, hdc dec across next two stitches*.
Repeat to the end.

17　Repeat round 16.

18 Repeat round 16.

19 Ch2 *hdc in next stitch, hdc dec in following stitch*.

20 Ch2, hdc in each st.

21 Repeat round 20.

22 Repeat round 20.

Did you know?

Prince, Liam Neeson, Iggy Azalea and one of the authors of this very book, Sonia, were all born on 7 June!

23 Weave in the ends and you are ready to wear!

Did you know?

In 2017, Pantone released a colour called Love Symbol #2. Pantone said "The colour pays tribute to Prince's indelible mark on music, art, fashion and culture."

YOU GOT THE *Scrapbook*

A cut-out-and-keep paper Prince

Prince really could do everything, so where do we start when putting together a scrapbook of his musical talents?

He was a prolific writer, composer, producer, singer and musician and he famously played 27 instruments. But it was the guitar at which he was the most prodigiously skilled. Search any list of the best ever guitar solos and you'll be sure to find a Prince performance in there.

Perhaps the most emotionally charged was his performance of the Beatles' hit "While My Guitar Gently Weeps" at the induction of George Harrison into the Rock & Roll Hall of Fame, where he takes the final solo and makes it sublimely his own, alongside George's son Dhani and Tom Petty.

Our scrapbook just wouldn't be complete without our very own paper tribute to Prince and his incredible shredding cred.

YOU WILL NEED:

- Coloured card (we used bright blue, pale blue, white, black, cream and brown, but you can use other colours if you like)
- Self-healing cutting mat
- Craft knife with blade
- Masking tape
- Glue stick or double-sided tape
- Prince template printed on paper (see page 83)

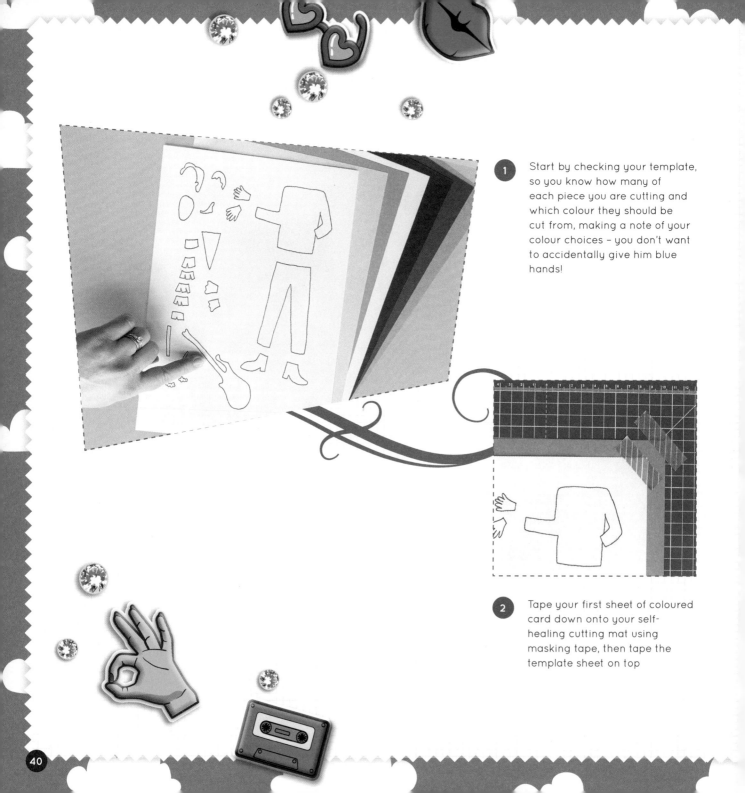

1 Start by checking your template, so you know how many of each piece you are cutting and which colour they should be cut from, making a note of your colour choices – you don't want to accidentally give him blue hands!

2 Tape your first sheet of coloured card down onto your self-healing cutting mat using masking tape, then tape the template sheet on top

3 Using your craft knife, cut out the pieces you've decided should be that colour (e.g. cut the pieces labelled "white" from the white card). You will cut through both the template sheet and the coloured card underneath.

For advice about cutting, see the Top Tips box in the Snow in April project.

4 Simply repeat the process with the other sheets of coloured card, until you have cut out all the pieces on the template sheet.

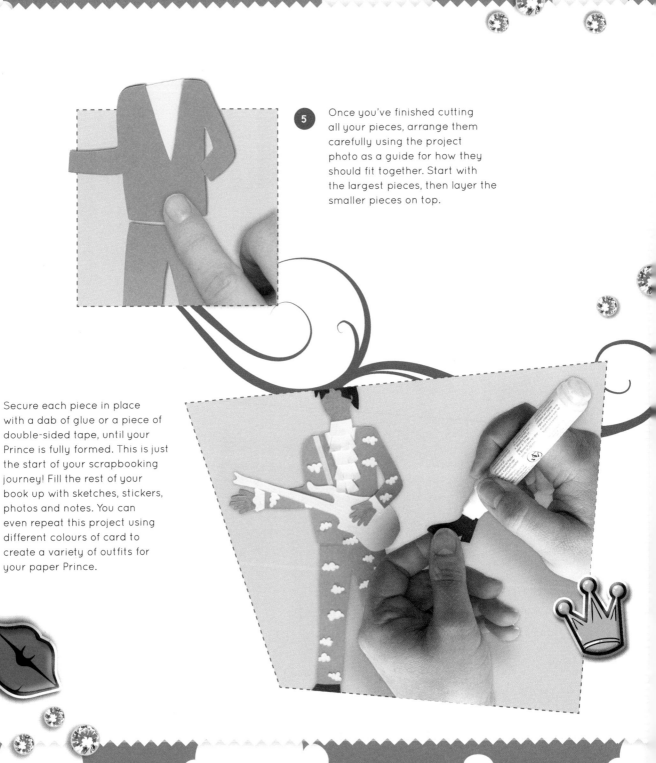

5 Once you've finished cutting all your pieces, arrange them carefully using the project photo as a guide for how they should fit together. Start with the largest pieces, then layer the smaller pieces on top.

6 Secure each piece in place with a dab of glue or a piece of double-sided tape, until your Prince is fully formed. This is just the start of your scrapbooking journey! Fill the rest of your book up with sketches, stickers, photos and notes. You can even repeat this project using different colours of card to create a variety of outfits for your paper Prince.

NO PARTICULAR Sign

Tribute

Prince performed his own signature spin on some incredible tracks, including Radiohead's "Creep" and Bob Dylan's "All Along the Watchtower".

YOU WILL NEED:

- Piece of wood (we used a wooden chopping board that we cut to size)
- Sandpaper
- Design template printed on paper (see page 85)
- Carbon paper
- Masking tape
- Pencil
- Acrylic paints in purple and white
- Paintbrush

Signpost your Prince fandom

If you're a band or an artist, how do you signpost your admiration for another artist's work? By covering it, of course.

However, Prince adamantly defended the rights of artists to control the use of their creative output, fighting to keep his own work off streaming services and often refusing permission for covers, most famously denying the Foo Fighters' request to cover "Darling Nikki". He allegedly said, "When I want to hear new music, I go make some".

Then, in a mysterious gesture not quite understood by anyone, he covered the Foo Fighters' song "Have It All" at his legendary 2007 Super Bowl appearance. The story goes that the band preferred the Purple One's rendition.

1 Make sure your piece of wood is clean and smooth ready to paint on. If there are any rough patches, you can use a piece of sandpaper to smooth them out.

2 Lay a piece of carbon paper on the wood, then lay your template on top. Secure in place with masking tape.

3 Trace over the outlines of the design with the pencil, to transfer the design onto your piece of wood. Be careful not to press too hard.

4 Remove the carbon paper and template, and check to make sure the design has transferred on to the wood properly. If there are any gaps or faint areas just go over them very lightly with the pencil.

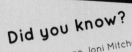

Did you know?

Prince was a huge Joni Mitchell fan. The singer spotted him in the front row at one of her concerts, and he regularly sent her fan letters. He even covered her song "A Case of You".

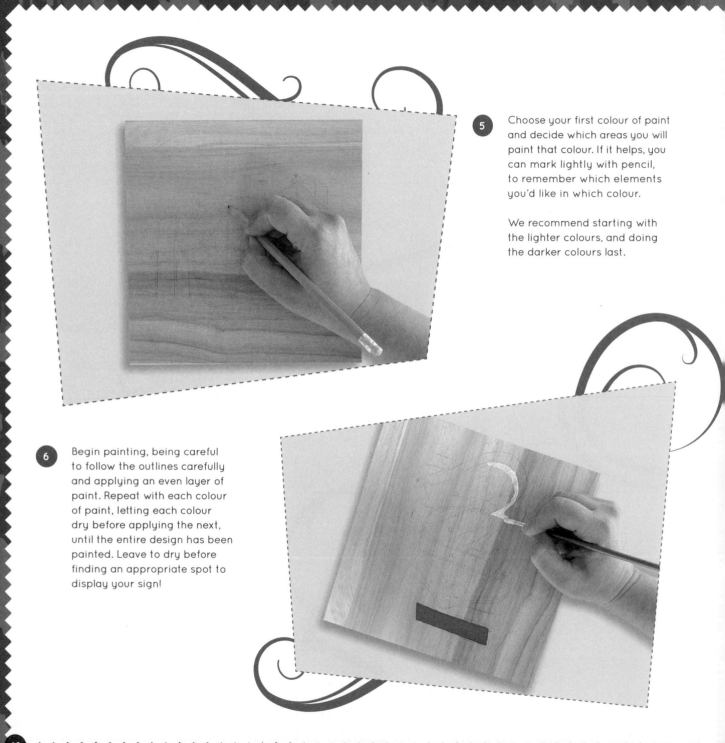

5 Choose your first colour of paint and decide which areas you will paint that colour. If it helps, you can mark lightly with pencil, to remember which elements you'd like in which colour.

We recommend starting with the lighter colours, and doing the darker colours last.

6 Begin painting, being careful to follow the outlines carefully and applying an even layer of paint. Repeat with each colour of paint, letting each colour dry before applying the next, until the entire design has been painted. Leave to dry before finding an appropriate spot to display your sign!

Snow IN APRIL

YOU WILL NEED:

- Wooden embroidery hoop
- White acrylic paint
- Paintbrush
- Two to three copies of the snowflake template printed on paper (see page 87)
- Coloured card (we used different shades of blue)
- Scissors
- Self-healing cutting mat
- Craft knife with blade
- Masking tape
- Glue gun
- Ribbon

This paper snowflake wreath is a delicate memento

It's said that the song "Sometimes It Snows in April" was recorded exactly 31 years to the day before Prince himself died.

A tragic tale in itself, the song tells the story of the death of Prince's character Christopher Tracy in his self-directed film *Under the Cherry Moon* and many of Prince's fans now view it as the ultimate eulogy to the singer.

The song has been covered by the American artist D'Angelo, UK band the Futureheads, Australian singer-songwriter Gotye, and many others. It may never have been released as a single, but on his death it charted in many countries around the world.

So take a little time to remember one of Prince's most beautiful songs as you carefully cut this paper snowflake wreath. We've tried to keep it spare and unfussy, just like the song, and we leave it to you to find the love in creating and assembling it.

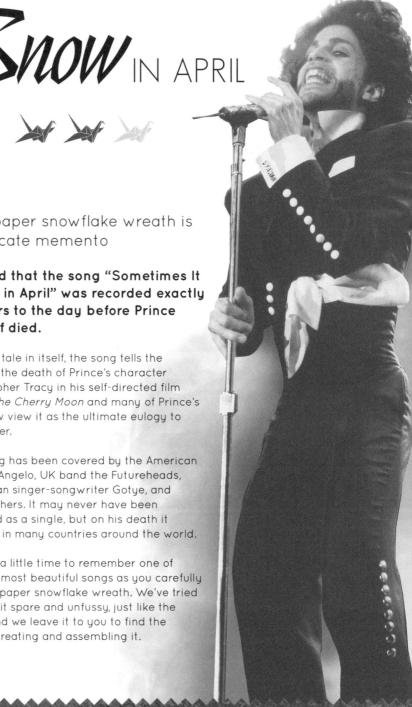

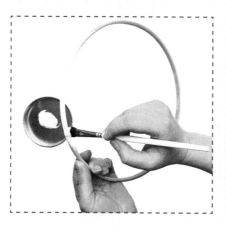

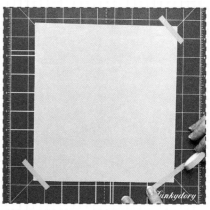

1 Start by taking apart your embroidery hoop, and painting the inner hoop white all over. Allow to dry while you move on to the next steps of the project.

2 Tape your first sheet of coloured card on to your self-healing cutting mat using masking tape.

3 Choose two or three snowflakes to cut out of your first colour of card, and roughly cut these away from the rest of the template.

4 Tape your first templates over your coloured card – you will be cutting through both the template and the coloured card at the same time. You want to press just hard enough that your knife cuts through both the template and the coloured card underneath. It may take a couple of attempts to get the amount of pressure right.

5 Once you've cut out the snowflakes you want from the first colour, repeat with your other colours of card until you have 8–12 snowflakes cut out.

6 Arrange your snowflakes on your painted embroidery hoop, mixing up the colours and sizes of snowflakes until you're happy with how they are placed.

When cutting a corner, always start from the corner and cut away from it, as this will ensure the blade cuts right into the corner without going too far.

Curves can be tricky to cut, so take your time. Don't try to cut the whole thing in one go, and keep turning your work as you cut.

TOP TIPS FOR CUTTING

Hold your craft knife in the same way you'd hold a pen, making sure the blade is at roughly a 45-degree angle to the paper you are cutting.

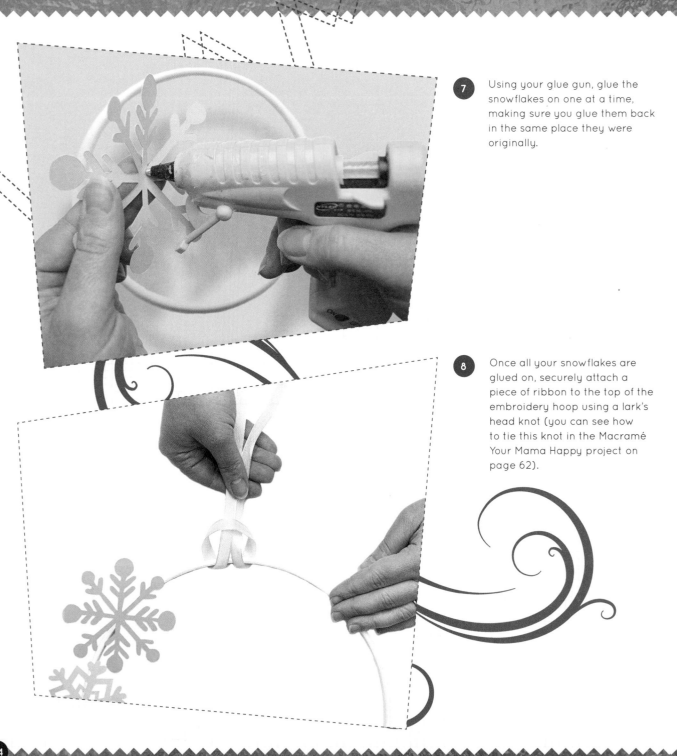

7. Using your glue gun, glue the snowflakes on one at a time, making sure you glue them back in the same place they were originally.

8. Once all your snowflakes are glued on, securely attach a piece of ribbon to the top of the embroidery hoop using a lark's head knot (you can see how to tie this knot in the Macramé Your Mama Happy project on page 62).

Child prodigy

Prince reputedly wrote his first song at the age of seven, titled "Machine". Prior to this, the young Prince learned his first song on the piano – the Batman theme tune.

YOUR EXTRA TIME AND YOUR *Stitch*

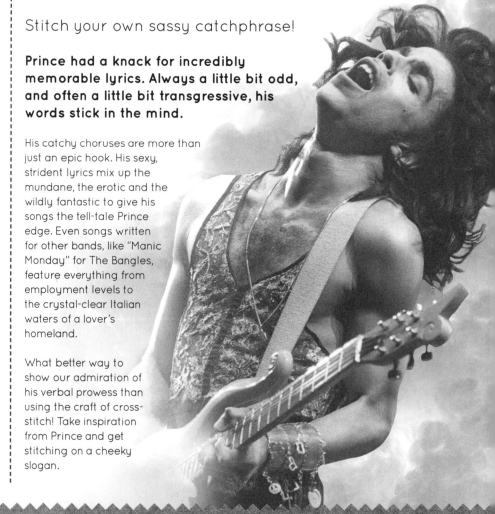

Stitch your own sassy catchphrase!

Prince had a knack for incredibly memorable lyrics. Always a little bit odd, and often a little bit transgressive, his words stick in the mind.

His catchy choruses are more than just an epic hook. His sexy, strident lyrics mix up the mundane, the erotic and the wildly fantastic to give his songs the tell-tale Prince edge. Even songs written for other bands, like "Manic Monday" for The Bangles, feature everything from employment levels to the crystal-clear Italian waters of a lover's homeland.

What better way to show our admiration of his verbal prowess than using the craft of cross-stitch! Take inspiration from Prince and get stitching on a cheeky slogan.

YOU WILL NEED:

- Aida 18-count cross-stitch fabric
- Embroidery hoop
- Cross-stitch needles
- Embroidery scissors
- Embroidery thread (we used different shades of purple)
- Cross-stitch pattern printed on paper (see page 89)

SO TONIGHT i'M GONNA PARTY

1 Start by preparing your hoop – loosen the screw at the top and take apart the two pieces.

2 Lay your piece of Aida on top of the inner hoop, then replace the outer hoop and tighten the screw fastening. Make sure the Aida is pulled tight in the hoop – it should be almost like a drum!

3 Separate your embroidery thread – each piece of thread is made of six strands, and you need to separate them into two lots of three strands each.

Do this by slowly pulling the piece of embroidery thread apart, allowing it to untwist as you go. Don't rush and pull it apart too quickly, as the thread can bunch up and become knotted.

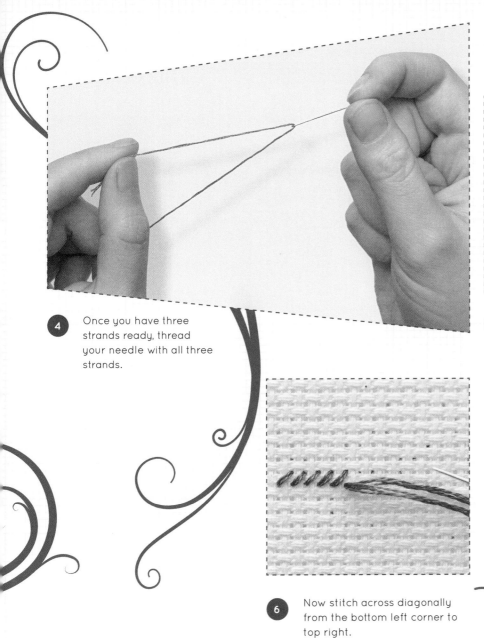

4 Once you have three strands ready, thread your needle with all three strands.

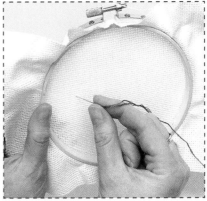

5 You don't need to tie a knot at the end of your thread. Simply push your needle through from the back, in the bottom left of where your first stitch will be, making sure you leave a short tail of thread at the back.

6 Now stitch across diagonally from the bottom left corner to top right.

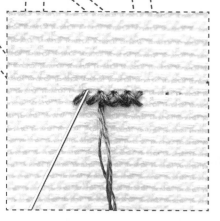 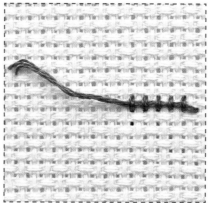 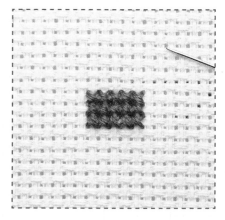

7 Once you've finished this row of stitches, go back and stitch the other half of the X, from the bottom right corner to the top left.

8 Continue across the row, stitching the first half of each stitch type. Keep your tail trapped at the back with each stitch.

9 Repeat this process for each stitch, following the pattern to make sure you stitch the correct number of stitches to form the letters. Each black square on the pattern represents one cross stitch.

We recommend marking off each stitch or row of stitches as you go, so you don't lose track.

We used a different shade of purple thread for each word, but you can stitch them in any colours you like!

Video:

Macramé YOUR MAMA HAPPY

YOU WILL NEED:

- One length of 5 mm cotton cord (we used Bobbiny), 40 cm (about 16 inches) long
- 30-cm (12-inch) piece of wooden dowel
- 12 lengths of 5 mm cotton cord (we used Bobbiny), each 5 m (5½ yards) long
- Pair of scissors

...with this sensational wall hanging

Prince had a phenomenal work ethic. By the time he was 19, he'd produced, arranged, composed and performed two studio albums.

He went on to create a total of 39 studio albums and four live albums. But that wasn't by any means the end of his creative output. Some of the most successful songs by artists including Kenny Rogers, Sheena Easton, Sinéad O'Connor and The Bangles were penned by Prince, and he was the driving force behind the Minneapolis music scene that emerged in the 1980s. He was forever reaching for the next achievement.

Your mamas would definitely be impressed to see you reviving the 1970s art of macramé. Try these basic knots and create a wall hanging to make somebody proud!

A Knotty Art

It's thought that the macramé technique began in the thirteenth century, when weavers in the Arab world used a system of knots to tie up the loose ends of yarn and thread on textiles that had been loomed by hand. The Moorish conquest brought the art to the West, and it took off with a diverse crowd – everyone from sailors and housewives to the aristocracy.

2

Lark's head: step 1
Take your first 5-metre (5½ -yard) piece of cord and fold it in half. Hang the folded cord over the dowel, with the folded loop facing away from you.

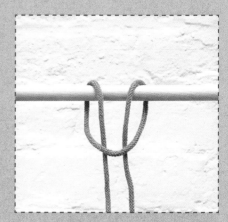

3

Lark's head: step 2
Take the long part of the folded cord (without the folded loop in it) and thread through the looped part of the cord in a downward direction.

1

Setting up your dowel
Begin by taking your short piece of cord and tying one end to each end of your wooden dowel. This will allow you to hang it up while you work. Find somewhere you can stand or sit with the dowel suspended in front of you. We like to stand a dining chair on a table and hang our work from that.

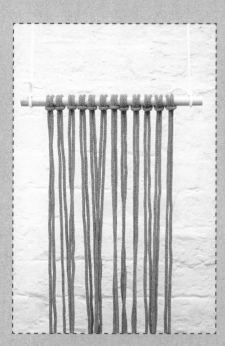

4 **Lark's head: step 3**
Pull downwards on the cord to tighten up and create your lark's head knot. Repeat Lark's head steps 1-3 with each of your 12 pieces of cord to create a neat row of lark's head knots. You are now ready to start your wall hanging!

5 **Spiral: step 1**
We are going to start with a row of half knot spirals which are our personal favourite macramé knot (don't tell the others, we don't want to hurt their feelings). In this project we will work with two sets of cords at a time, totalling four cords. The middle two cords are your filler cords, and the outer cords are your left working cord and right working cord. Take your left cord and make an L shape with it on top of the other cords. Place the right cord on top of the horizontal part of the L shape.

6 **Spiral: step 2**
Take the right cord behind all the other cords, and bring it out to the front through the gap created by the L between the left cord and the filler cords – keep hold of your left and right cords!

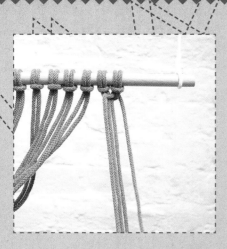

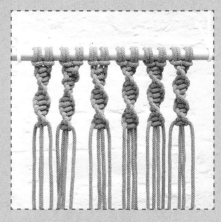

7 **Spiral: step 3**
Tighten the knot by holding the filler cords still and pulling the left and right cords in an upward motion until it reaches the top. This is your first half-knot spiral!

8 **Spiral: step 4**
Staying on the same set of four cords, repeat Spiral steps 1–3 to tie 11 more half-knot spirals.

9 **Spiral: step 5**
Once you have tied a few half-knot spirals it will start to spiral – don't worry about straightening it out each time, just let it spin. Whichever cord ends up on the left will become your left working cord, as this knot is totally reversible. To count how many knots you have tied, count the horizontal bars running across the middle of the spiral. Once you have completed your first spiral, take the next set of four cords and tie another 12 half-knot spirals using them. Repeat with each set of four cords until you have six beautiful spirals!

Take it up a notch

Macramé plant hangers are back with a vengeance – you can easily transfer the skills picked up in this project to create your very own hangers. Although only a handful of different knots to learn – once you've nailed these, you can create plant hangers galore and give your home a groovy 1970s vibe.

10 **Square: step 1**
We are now going to learn to tie a square knot, which is made in two halves. The good news is the first half of a square knot is identical to a half-knot spiral which you have already mastered! So take your first set of four cords (the ones you tied your first half-knot spiral with) and repeat Spiral: steps 1–3, but don't tighten the knot all the way up to your spiral. Leave a gap of about two inches.

11 **Square: step 2**
Once you have tied the first half of your square knot we are going to make the second half, which is the reverse of what we have just done. Start by making a back to front L shape with the right cord, across the two central cords, and then bring the left cord over on top of the horizontal part of the L shape.

12 **Square: step 3**
Take the left cord behind all the cords, and bring it out through the gap created by the backwards L of the right cord. Tighten up in the same way as for the spiral knot, holding the filler cords still and pulling the left and right cords in an upward motion. Don't pull too tightly as this may distort your knot. Congratulations, you've now tied a square knot!

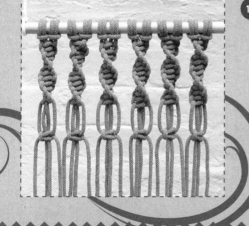

13 **Square: row 1**
Repeat this process with each set of four cords, tying one square knot with each group of cords. The trick to making your work look neat and professional is to make sure each square knot is in line with the previous one, and the gap between each spiral and square knot is identical.

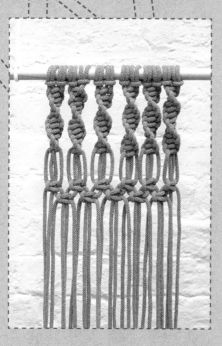

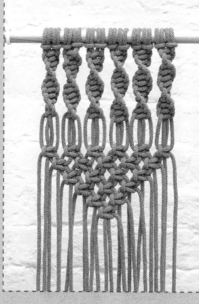

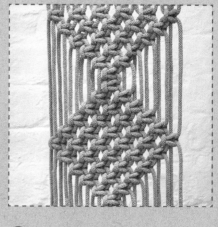

16 **Triangles**

To make a regular triangle underneath, start by tying another single square knot directly underneath your last single square knot. Then bring in two cords from the left and two cords from the right, and use these to tie another row of square knots (there should be two knots in this row.) Then bring in another two cords from each side and repeat the process, so each time you should be tying one more knot on each row, until on the final row, you tie six knots. Follow this with a row of five knots, then four, three, two and one, so you end up with a square diamond shape.

14 **Square: row 2**

We are going to make a triangle shape with our square knots, so once you have completed your first row of square knots (there should be six of them) take the two cords on the left of your work, and the two cords on the right of your work, and tuck them up and over your dowel out of the way. You won't use them for the next row. Now take what is now the first four cords and tie a square knot with them. This square knot should sit directly beneath and between the first two square knots on the row above.

15 **Square: rows 3–6**

Repeat with each group of four cords until you have five square knots in the row. Continue this process for a further four rows, each time taking away two cords from the left and two from the right. This should mean that with each row you are tying one less square knot, until on the final row you only tie one knot. You should now have an upside-down triangle.

17 **Finished!**

To complete your wall hanging, tie a regular triangle underneath your diamond, and finish with a final set of half knot spirals. All that's left now is to trim the ends of your work to the length you'd like, and then find somewhere to hang your wall hanging.

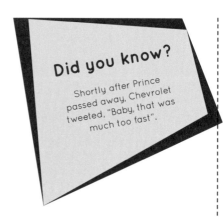

Whittle RED CROCHET HOOK

YOU WILL NEED:

- A piece of wood roughly the size of a crochet hook. You can forage for a nice twig or branch that's straight. What size you choose depends on the size of hook you want to make!
- Hand saw
- Whittling knife
- Red paint suitable for wood (acrylic paint or a non-toxic gloss paint)
- Sandpaper (1 coarse sheet, 1 fine sheet)

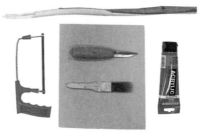

Woodwork a love that's gonna last

Prince wasn't one to shy away from sex in his lyrics, and perhaps the reason some of his early songs weren't hits was because they were so explicitly erotic.

But sexuality was at the core of his being, so it's fitting that his first Top-10 US hit was all about a one-night stand.

"Little Red Corvette", on first listen, sounds like a song about a car – but in fact it's all about the briefest of romances. It's full of innuendo, but the meaning was veiled just enough to get the song the radio play it deserved, with nothing too overtly naughty in its joyful, sing-a-long chorus. By 2001, the song was so well loved that Chevrolet was happy to associate with it, putting up a series of billboards reading, "They don't write songs about Volvos." Have a try at whittling this racy red crochet hook – aim for a sleek and smooth silhouette, just like the Corvette that inspired it.

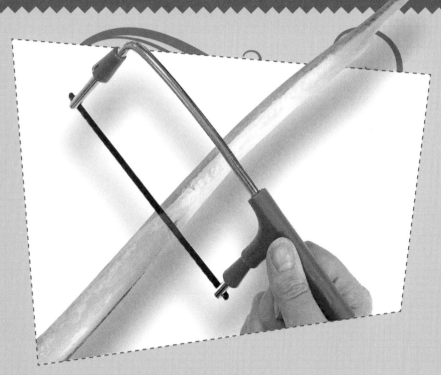

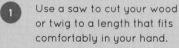
Use a saw to cut your wood or twig to a length that fits comfortably in your hand.

2 Hold the wood in one hand, pointing away from you and downwards. Push the whittling knife downwards and away along the surface of the wood, so it peels off a top layer. Make sure your hands are behind the knife, out of harm's way.

Dream lover

The lyrics to "Little Red Corvette" came to Prince in a dream, when he was napping in the backseat of singer Lisa Coleman's car.

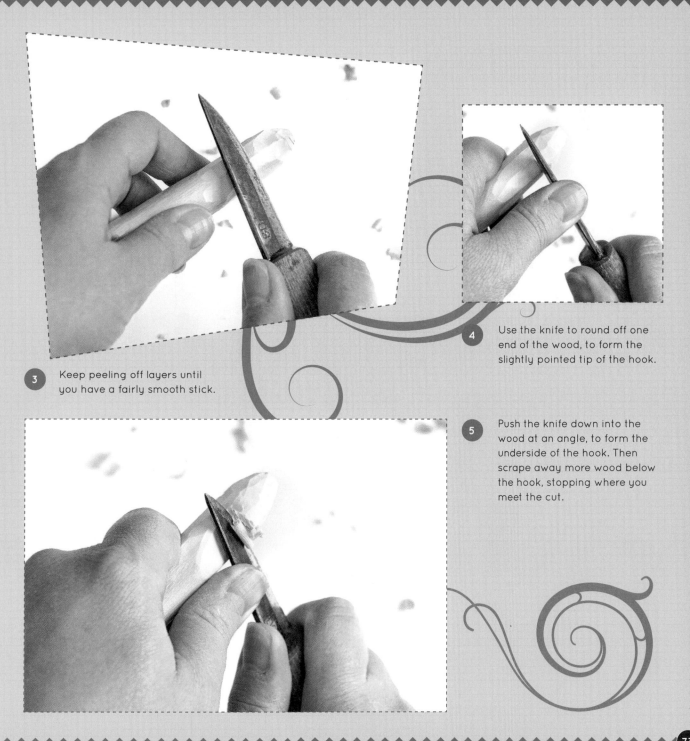

3 Keep peeling off layers until you have a fairly smooth stick.

4 Use the knife to round off one end of the wood, to form the slightly pointed tip of the hook.

5 Push the knife down into the wood at an angle, to form the underside of the hook. Then scrape away more wood below the hook, stopping where you meet the cut.

6 Keep cutting and scraping until you have formed a rough hook shape.

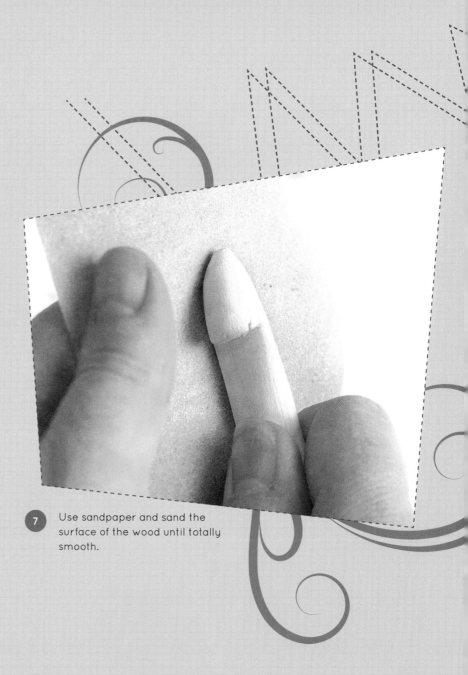

7 Use sandpaper and sand the surface of the wood until totally smooth.

8 Finally, paint the handle of your crochet hook red and leave to dry. Use!

Templates

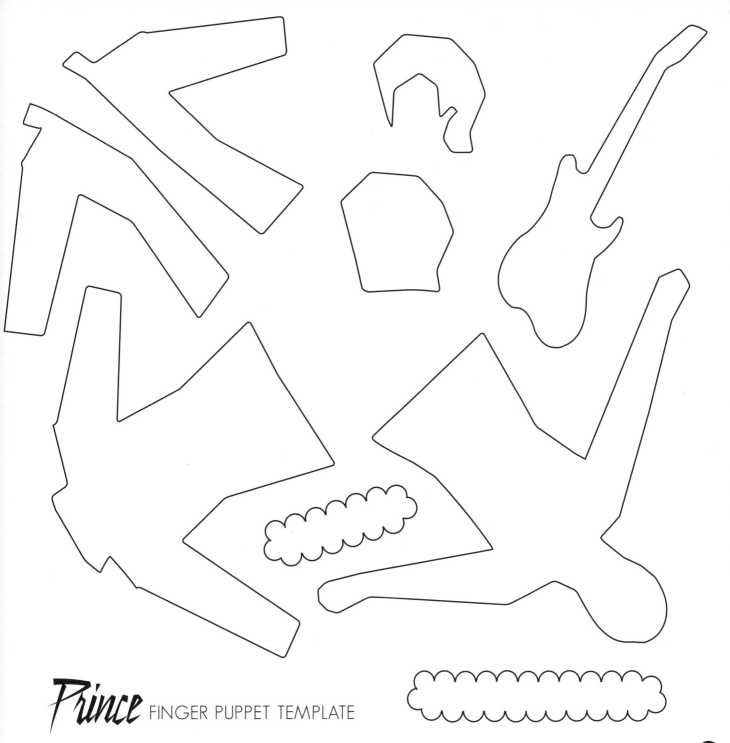

Prince FINGER PUPPET TEMPLATE

I WOULD *Dye* FOR YOU TEMPLATE

YOU GOT THE
Scrapbook TEMPLATE

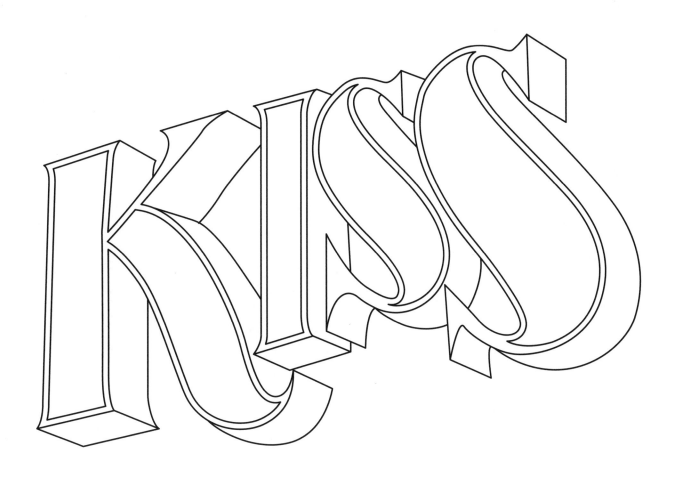

 NO PARTICULAR TEMPLATE

Snow IN APRIL
TEMPLATE

SO TONIGHT I'M GONNA PARTY

YOUR EXTRA TIME
AND YOUR  *Stitch* TEMPLATE

89

7 June 1958

Prince Rogers Nelson is born in Minneapolis, Minnesota, to a jazz singer mother and musician father

October 1979

His second album, *Prince*, is released, and certified Platinum

May 1983

"Little Red Corvette" goes to #6 in the charts, and the video is one of the first by a black artist to feature in regular rotation on MTV

July 1984

The movie *Purple Rain* is released one week before the album of the same name, which sold 13 million copies in the US alone

April 1978

Prince's debut album, *For You*, is released and charts at #163

October 1982

1999 sells over five million copies worldwide, cementing the Purple One's status as a megastar

July 1994

Prince tops the charts for the first time with "When Doves Cry"

March 1985

He wins the Best Original Score Academy Award for the *Purple Rain* soundtrack

Timeline

April 1986

"Kiss" tops the US charts, while the Prince-penned "Manic Monday" by The Bangles takes the #2 spot

May 1988

Lovesexy becomes his first album to top the UK charts

March 2004

Prince is inducted into The Rock and Roll Hall of Fame

April 2016

Prince dies at his Paisley Park estate, aged 57

March 1987

Prince's ninth album *Sign o' the Times* is released

October 1992

The Love Symbol features on an album cover, and in 1993 Prince changes his name to the symbol, giving him the freedom to control his creative output while "Prince" was trademarked and owned by Warner Bros.

May 2000

Finally, Prince's name belongs to him again when his Warner Bros. contract comes to an end

February 2007

The Purple One's Super Bowl halftime show went down in history as the greatest ever, ending with a rapturous performance of "Purple Rain", performed in torrential rain

Index

Page numbers in *italic* refer to photographs

A
acceptance 20
"All Along the Watchtower" 44
"Another Lonely Christmas" 50
Around the World in a Day 32
The Artist Formerly Known as Prince 20
Azalea, Iggy 36

B
Bangles 20, 56, 62, 91
batik 20
Batman 56
Beatles 38

C
"A Case of You" 48
Chevrolet 70
Christmas 50
Coleman, Lisa 72
"Creep" 44
cutting tips 53

D
D'Angelo 50
"Darling Nikki" 44
Dylan, Bob 44

E
Easton, Sheena 62

F
Foo Fighters 44
France, Marie 18
Futureheads 50

G
galaxy room 10
gender fluidity 20

Gotye 50
Grand Central 14

H
Harrison, Dhani 38
Harrison, George 38
"Have It All" 44

I
"I Feel For You" 20
individuality 20

K
Khan, Chaka 20
"Kiss" 91
knots 64, 66

L
"Little Red Corvette" 70, 72, 90
London Craft Club videos 32, 62
Love Symbol 20, *21, 22, 23, 24, 25, 81,* 91
Love Symbol #2 38
Lovesexy 91
Luce, Lizz 20

M
"Machine" 56
macramé, history of 64
"Manic Monday" 20, 56, 91
Minneapolis Civic Center 50
Minneapolis music scene 62
Mitchell, Joni 48
Monson, Mitch 20
Moorish conquest 64
MTV 90

N
Neeson, Liam 36
Nelson, Prince Rogers *11, 14, 20, 26, 38, 44, 50, 62, 76,* 90, *96*

albums of 14, 26, 32, 90, 91
birth of 90
death of 91
as "Love Symbol" 20, 91
movies of 14, 18, 26, 50, 90
songs covered by 38, 44
songs of (other artists) 20, 56, 91
songs of (own) 26, 32, 44, 50, 56, 70, 72, 90, 91
1970s vibe 66
1999 90
"Nothing Compares 2 U" 20

O
O'Connor, Sinéad 20, 62

P
Paisley Park 10, 91
Pantone 38
Petty, Tom 38
Prince *see* The Artist Formerly Known as Prince; Love Symbol; Nelson, Prince Rogers
Prince (album) 90
Purple Rain 90
Purple Rain (album) 14, 26, 90
Purple Rain (movie) 14, 18, 26, 90
"Purple Rain" (single) 26, 91

Q
QR codes 32, 62

R
Radio Head 44
"Raspberry Beret" 32
Rock & Roll Hall of Fame 38, 91
Rogers, Kenny 62
ruffled shirt 14, 18, *18, 19,* 26, *26,* 44

S
self-expression 10
1970s vibe 66
sexuality 20, 70
Sign o' the Times 91
signature look 10
"Sometimes It Snows In April" 50
Sonia 36
Super Bowl 2007 44, 91

T
templates:
finger puppet 79
Kiss 85
Love Symbol 81
scrapbook 83
snow 87
stitch 89
timeline (1958–2016) 90–1
Tracy, Christopher (character) 50
transgressiveness 56

U
Under the Cherry Moon 50

W
Warner Bros. 20, 91
Wells, Louis 18
"When Doves Cry" 90
"While My Guitar Gently Weeps" 38
work ethic 62

Y
For You 90